To Saralyit !
Enjoy & lea

Enjoy

From

Mr Delgadillo

SAMSON

LAST OF THE CALIFORNIA GRIZZLIES

ROBERT M. McCLUNG

illustrated by Bob Hines

Linnet Books

Hamden, Connecticut 1992

Published 1992 as a Linnet Book,
an imprint of The Shoe String Press, Inc.
Hamden, Connecticut 06514

Library of Congress Cataloging-in-Publication Data

McClung, Robert M.
Samson, last of the California grizzlies /
Robert M. McClung : illustrated by Bob Hines.
p.   cm.
Originally published: New York : Morrow, 1973.
Summary: During the first nine years of his
life a California grizzly struggles for
survival against the ever increasing
threat of humans in the Sierra Nevada.
1. Grizzly bear—Juvenile fiction.
[1. Grizzly bear—Fiction. 2. Bears—Fiction.]
I. Hines, Bob, ill. II. Title.
PZ10.3.M4545Sam   1992   91-33350   [Fic]—dc20
ISBN 0-208-02327-5

The paper in this publication meets the minimum
requirements of American National Standard for
Information Sciences—Permanence of Paper for
Printed Library Materials, ANSI Z39.48—1984 ∞

Samson: Last of the California Grizzlies is
Number Five in the Animal Life Cycle Series.

The Animal Life Cycle Series:
1. *Major: The Story of a Black Bear*
2. *Thor: Last of the Sperm Whales*
3. *Shag: Last of the Plains Buffalo*
4. *Black Jack: Last of the Big Alligators*
5. *Samson: Last of the California Grizzlies*

Printed in the United States of America

CONTENTS

1 THE GRIZZLY DEN

A chickaree chattered nervously from its perch high in a pine tree. Then a magpie flashed over the clearing shrieking its alarm call. *Quek — quek — quek — quek!*

A moment later a big bear emerged from the underbrush and started to amble across the meadow. The huge beast paid no attention to the cries of the squirrel and bird as it padded across the clearing. She wasn't after them. A light snow was beginning to fall on this morning in November, 1840, and the bear was heading for the winter den that she had prepared some weeks before.

Big for a female, the bear stood more than three feet high at the shoulder and weighed nearly seven hundred pounds. Her large size, pronounced shoulder hump, and the concave profile of her face clearly marked her as a grizzly and not a black bear. Her color was typical of the California grizzly — an overall yellow-brown, with darker back and feet.

The big bear plodded steadily onward, following a smooth, narrow path that countless generations of grizzlies before her had worn through the western foothills of the Sierra Nevada. In the year 1840 grizzlies were very common in this region. California was a province of Mexico at that time and still mostly wilderness. Apart from primitive Indian villages, its only human settlements were the string of Spanish missions along the coast and the great ranchos in the central plains.

Behind the bear, the land sloped away to the west in countless rolling hills and dales toward the San Joaquin Valley. Ahead the hills grew steeper and more rugged. For much of the way the she-bear followed a small river that foamed and burbled around jagged boulders as it hurried toward the distant lowlands. On either side were stands of dense brush, or chaparral, broken by scattered mountain clearings carpeted with dry brown grass. Here and there were clumps of aspens or groves of sugar or yellow pines. Far ahead of the bear, and over everything else, the snow-covered peaks of the Sierra Nevada cut the sky with their jagged summits.

On the grizzly padded, covering mile after mile as the hours passed. By noon the sky was hidden by a swiftly moving mass of gray clouds from which snow was beginning to fall in earnest. The big flakes swirled thick and heavy around the bear, quickly covering the ground and coating the trees. Undaunted, she plodded onward through the storm and by late afternoon had traveled nearly twenty miles.

As dusk began to settle, she came at last to a wooded canyon with steep slopes carved thousands of years before by glaciers. Turning into it, she

came after a few moments to the end of her journey —a large hole on the north-facing slope under the roots of a giant old cedar. It was the entrance to the den where the grizzly would spend the winter. After sniffing at the opening, she went in.

Barely large enough to admit the bear, the den entrance sloped slightly downward for eight feet, then widened into a chamber some seven feet across and four feet high. The floor was covered with a thick layer of dried leaves and pine branches, which she had dragged in after digging the underground room. Stirring up the bedding with her paw, the bear turned round and round to mold her nest, then settled into it with a sigh. Soon she was sleeping. She would not leave the den until spring came once again to the Sierra Nevada. Outside, the first big snow of the season continued to fall, and in a few minutes her tracks were covered.

November passed, then December, and the new year of 1841 dawned. Winter snow drifted deep over the den entrance, with only a small hole kept open by the warm breath of the sleeping bear. From time to time she stirred about and muttered softly to herself, for she did not sink into a deep deathlike trance during the long cold season as marmots and other true hibernators do. Her body temperature remained relatively high; her breathing and heartbeat, although slowed down, were strong and regular.

During the third week in January the bear gave birth to two tiny cubs. No bigger than rats, the two helpless infants seemed like unfinished creatures. Their eyes were closed, their ears tiny and wrinkled. The cubs' feet ended in pinlike claws and their bodies were almost naked, covered only by a barely visible sprinkling of fine hair. Samson, the male cub, weighed a pound and a half and measured just ten inches from the tip of his nose to the end of his stub tail. He was bigger than his sister.

The newborn cubs squirmed and mewed and snuggled close to their huge dozing mother. They

nuzzled her furry underparts, groping and searching until each found a nipple. The old bear had six nipples in all—four on her breast and two between her hind legs. As the young ones nursed, the old bear roused from her sleep and drowsily licked them clean.

Day by day the cubs grew bigger and stronger. Silky gray-brown fur soon began to cover their roly-poly bodies, and when they were about two weeks old their dark brown eyes opened. By mid-March the cubs were as big as rabbits. They were lively and alert, but their whole world was limited by the dark walls of the den and by their mother — the source of food and warmth.

In late March they began to hear the steady drip, drip, drip of melting snow, and finally a day came when a ray of sunlight shone like a beacon outside the entrance of the den. Every day their

mother became more restless and wide-awake. One morning she yawned broadly, then shuffled to the front of the den and peered outside. After a moment she grunted at Samson and his sister, ordering them to stay where they were. Then she crawled out and was gone.

The grizzly cubs huddled together in the strange emptiness of the nest. To Samson, the den seemed very big without his mother in it. The she-bear returned after several hours, however, and with his mother's giant warm body close to him Samson once again felt secure.

During the next several weeks Samson's mother left the den a number of times without taking the cubs with her. But one morning in mid-April she called to the cubs, telling them to follow her.

Shoving his sister aside in his eagerness, Samson scrambled up the entranceway. He shook his head and blinked at the blinding light. Then slowly and cautiously, he stepped outside, followed by his sister.

2   A CUB IN THE SIERRA NEVADA

The earth felt damp under Samson's feet, but warm from the rays of the spring sun. Samson smelled many strange odors around him—the musty scent of a rotting log, the fresh smell of growing plants. He swatted experimentally at a pile of dried leaves and heard them rustle. A shiny black beetle scurried out from under one of them, and Samson shied back in surprise.

A chipmunk chirred as it streaked past him and into a nearby stand of manzanita. The shrubs were so thick and dense that Samson could not see through them. Farther away two yellow pines towered into the blue of the sky like giant twin sentinels. Above them soared a golden eagle.

Grunting to the cubs, the old bear started down the slope, and the cubs followed close behind her. Samson and his sister sniffed at patches of old snow, felt its cold wetness against their noses. They rolled in the snow, then jumped up to shake it off in a spray of grainy white flakes. Samson rubbed against the rough bark of the nearest yellow pine, pungent with the odor of gum.

He watched while his mother dug spring bulbs and ate them. Then the big bear shifted a log, and a wood rat scurried out of it. Samson's mother killed the furry little rodent with a flick of her paw and bolted it down.

As they headed back to the den at sunset Samson listened to wolves howling mournfully in the distance. Safe in the familiar nest, he snuggled up to his mother and went to sleep.

16

After that time, the cubs went out with their mother every day, but at first she brought them back to the den to sleep. As they gained strength, they wandered farther and farther from the den. Soon the old bear took to bedding down with the cubs wherever they might be. One time they curled up under a sheltering ledge of rock, another time on a soft bed of pine needles at the base of a tree. Sometimes they simply lay down under the sheltering branches of a stand of chaparral.

The old bear ate these days as though she would never get enough. She dug hour after hour for bulbs of wild onions and lilies, and chomped them down with grunts of satisfaction. As clover and grass sprouted in the mountain meadows, she grazed on the tender green shoots, cropping them like a cow. She turned rocks over and lapped up the beetles and other insects beneath them with relish.

One sunny morning the old bear led the cubs to the banks of the river. The young ones watched as she waded into the shallows, heading for the ripples where the river narrowed. Suddenly her head flashed downward, then up with a fat, flopping trout in her jaws. Wading ashore, she ate the fish, smacking her lips over the last morsels. Then she walked into the stream again and caught another fish and still another.

Satisfied at last, she heaved a contented sigh, then lay down to doze and dry off in the sun while the cubs played nearby. Samson batted at a butterfly and sat down to watch a big crested woodpecker hammering at a tree trunk. After a few moments

he saw a strange bear — a big black one — ambling toward him, followed by two cubs. The strange bear was not a grizzly. She had a straight nose and lacked a shoulder hump. She was an American black bear.

Curious, Samson started to amble toward the two strange cubs. Suddenly he heard a warning whoof behind him. His mother was ordering him to come back. The big grizzly had risen and was lumbering toward the black bears, a growl sounding deep in her throat. The mother black bear gave

a startled snort, then quickly turned and headed back the way she had come, followed by her cubs. Samson's mother trailed them for a moment. Then she stopped, satisfied that her own cubs were safe.

The little grizzlies nursed many times each day and grew rapidly. By mid-May Samson weighed fifteen pounds, by early June nearly twenty-five. His body was rounded and plump. His outer fur was soft and silky, a smoky gray over a warm red-brown undercoat. His toes were tipped with sharp blue-white claws, but the smooth bare soles of his feet were soft as tanned deerskin.

As June approached, wild flowers splashed the Sierra Nevada with rainbows of color. Stands of blue lupines mixed with yellow poppies on the slopes, while columbine, daisies, and meadow-foam all brightened the clearings. In the woods tall orange and yellow lilies nodded over beds of ferns.

One day Samson and his sister explored a glade while their mother turned over rocks in search of mice and other tidbits. Suddenly they heard a loud

whoof. Looking up, Samson saw an enormous
grizzly bear watching them from the edge of the
woods. The big bear whoofed again, then headed
toward Samson's mother.

Shooing the cubs behind her, the she-bear
quickly positioned herself between them and the
giant bear. She growled a warning as the male

grizzly continued to walk toward her. She wanted nothing to do with him. When he was close beside her, she snarled and nipped his flank. Rebuffed, the male bear retreated a short distance and sat down. After a few moments he approached the she-bear once again, only to be rejected as before. Discouraged, he finally went away.

Calling the cubs to her, Samson's mother quickly moved off in the opposite direction. She would not accept a mate this year, when she had small cubs. A year from now the cubs would be old enough to take care of themselves, and she would be receptive.

The she-bear was not afraid of any of the big animals of the mountains — other bears, mountain lions, or wolves. Nor was she afraid of the few scattered bands of Indians who sometimes shared the slopes with her. There were a few animals, however, whose powers she respected.

One evening she and the cubs saw a group of little black-and-white animals with bushy tails — a family of skunks — coming down the trail toward them. Giving way, the big grizzly led Samson and his sister off to one side and let the skunks pass.

Several days later Samson was stalking a tiny lizard perched on a sunlit rock when he heard a strange whirring sound. A few feet away lay a

big snake, its flat plated head raised between the coils of its scaly body. The snake followed his movements with unblinking eyes, its forked tongue flicking rapidly in and out. The whirring noise came from the rattles on the snake's tail.

Samson stopped and watched the rattlesnake, his curiosity dampened by instinctive fear. Suddenly he heard his mother growl, then felt her huge paw sweeping him back and away from the

snake. Uncoiling, the reptile slithered into a crevice in the rocks and disappeared.

July came in hot and dry as the sun blazed down day after day. The cubs were still nursing, but now they began to sample solid foods as well. They ate blackberries, chokecherries, and other fruits of the mountain meadows. They smacked their lips over insects, as their mother did. Every day they tried some new food or other. One day it was nectar and grubs from a bumblebee's nest dug up by the old bear, the next day a crayfish or frog or the pulpy hips of wild roses. By mid-August, when he was seven months old, Samson weighed seventy pounds. Two months after, he weighed nearly a hundred and ten.

The old bear dug a new den that fall, and one cold day in late October she and the cubs retired into it for the winter. The season's first snowfall came that same night, a thick downfall that locked the upper slopes of the Sierra Nevada in a blanket of white for the next five months.

3   VAQUEROS AND REATAS

In mid-April the bears emerged from the den and took up the hunt for food once again. Now Samson and his sister were yearling bears. They still nursed, but they ranged far and wide with their mother and foraged for themselves much of the time. By late spring, when he was close to a year and a half old, Samson weighed almost 175 pounds and his sister 25 pounds less.

By early July the lush green look of the foothills in spring and early summer was beginning to disappear. The grass rippled golden brown in the meadows, and the roaring brooks of springtime were reduced to gurgling trickles. Sometimes Samson saw a thick haze of smoke on the lower slopes where Indians had set fires to keep the clearings open.

One afternoon he noticed clouds of dust in the distant lowlands and caught fleeting glimpses of many long-horned animals running together. He heard faint shouts intermixed with bellowing and watched as men on horseback galloped around the herd of milling cattle. The men on horseback were vaqueros — cowboys from a great rancho in the valley. They were rounding up a herd of long-horned Spanish cattle.

Samson's mother led the young bears into the nearby chaparral where they would be hidden. She had met similar horsemen in the past and didn't want to confront them again.

One afternoon several days later, the bears came upon a strong scent of meat at the edge of a wide clearing. They followed it to the center of the field. There lay the bloated carcass of a cow. A huge vulture, its bare orange head bobbing up and down, was tearing at the cow's throat. Two coyotes crouched at the other end of the body, tugging and snapping at a hind leg.

Samson's mother advanced with a growl. She wanted the meat for herself. The coyotes slowly retreated, their lips drawn back in snarls of disappointment. At a safe distance they stopped and sat down to wait their turn once again. The giant bird, a California condor, waddled away too. Spreading its great wings and pumping them, it hurried clumsily down the slope until it was airborne. Samson watched as it circled higher and higher, the flight feathers at the tips of its wings spread like fingers.

Samson's mother tore hungrily at the strong-smelling meat and ate her fill. As she gorged, the coyotes crept closer to watch and wait, their eyes shining in the gathering darkness. Finally finished,

the she-grizzly dragged the remainder of the carcass under a bushy stand of manzanita and scratched brush and earth over it. She would return to her cache at some future time.

At dusk the next evening, just twenty-four hours later, the she-bear and cubs came back. Scraping the debris away from the carcass, Samson's mother began to bolt down another meal of rotting beef.

Suddenly Samson heard shouts and the rapid tattoo of many hoofs pounding the dry earth. Six horses, three from either side, galloped out of the trees that bordered the clearing. Each horse carried a vaquero swinging a plaited rawhide reata, or lasso, over his head.

Vaqueros were expert horsemen. They loved any sport or activity — the more dangerous the better — that allowed them to show off their horsemanship and courage. One of their favorite amusements was to capture grizzly bears by lassoing them with their reatas. They often used the carcass of a cow as bait to attract the grizzlies to a suitable spot.

Samson watched with awe as the vaqueros galloped straight toward him, his mother, and his sister. There was no chance for the bears to escape the sudden attack. With a growl Samson's mother shooed the cubs into a small patch of nearby chaparral. Then she turned to face the vaqueros pounding down on her.

Peering out of the brush, Samson saw the shouting horsemen wheel toward his mother in the fading light, their looped reatas swishing around their heads. The old bear crouched in the open meadow with no sheltering bush or rock against which to take a stand. Closing in, the horses galloped around her in a thundering circle. Again and again the

31

besieged grizzly charged at one of them, and then at another. But each time the threatened horse and rider danced back while another charged her from the opposite direction.

Yipping with excitement, the vaqueros began to toss their reatas. One of the plaited loops swished

over the grizzly's muzzle, but with a quick toss of
her head she shook it off before the noose tightened.
She was still off-balance, however, when another
reata settled over her left foreleg. She swatted at
it with her right paw, but too late. The noose
tightened as the spirited horse pranced back away

from her. With a jerk she was rolled over on her back.

Snapping and snarling, she bit frantically at the reata, but before she could free herself, still another loop settled over her right hind leg. The successful vaquero yelped in triumph as he wheeled his horse away from her, drawing the reata taut. Now Samson's mother was held by a rope on either side.

Two other vaqueros quickly threw their reatas once more, and the ropes settled over the bear's two remaining free limbs. Soon she was pinned down by four ropes — each one tied to the saddle horn of a prancing mustang and stretched tight in a different direction.

With Samson's mother roped and on her back, the last two horsemen dismounted and advanced on her. Quickly and expertly they bound her legs together with their reatas, then tied her jaws with another piece of rawhide. She growled and struggled desperately as they worked, but soon she was thoroughly trussed up and helpless.

Working together, the vaqueros hoisted their heavy victim onto a bullock hide. Two of them attached ropes to the improvised drag and started to pull the bear behind their horses toward a two-wheeled oxcart, which had been concealed in the trees at the edge of the clearing. The other men set out to capture Samson and his sister. The light

was fast fading, and they wanted to catch the cubs as quickly as possible.

Samson whined with fright as the horsemen came toward the place where he and his sister were hiding. When the horses were almost on top of them, the cubs scooted out in a desperate dash for the nearest trees. Samson felt a reata brush against his back and slide away. Dodging, he ran on. A moment later a second rope hit his head, and he brushed it off with a flick of his paw.

Above the pounding hoofs he heard a shout of excitement behind him, and then a frightened bawl. His sister had been caught. Dodging and turning, Samson ran on. The edge of the forest was close, and only two vaqueros were following him. Another moment and he was among the trees. Plunging on in the enveloping darkness he reached a stand of prickly chaparral that the horsemen could not enter.

He had escaped, but not his mother or sister. Samson was alone.

4 THE VALLEY OF AHWANEE

Samson lay panting in the brush and listened to the shouts and curses of the vaqueros as they searched for him. Luckily they had no dogs with them. After a while the sounds of the horsemen faded away. Samson could hear nothing except the chirping of crickets in the warm night air and the howls of a distant coyote.

Several hours passed before the yearling bear mustered enough courage to creep back to the meadow to search for his mother. He bawled softly as he ran back and forth looking for her, but heard no comforting snort in reply. His mother and sister were gone. He did sniff out their scents, but soon lost them in a welter of other odors of men and horses and oxen.

Finally abandoning the search, Samson left the meadow where his mother and sister had been captured and struck off through the forest, heading for the higher slopes above him. During the next two days he traveled twenty-five miles or more, stopping only to eat some berries when he was hungry or to sleep in some protective brush.

By the third night he was far up the mountainside, and the country around him became ever more rugged. An eerie scream sounded from a canyon, signaling a prowling mountain lion, but the yearling bear paid no attention as he wandered onward. Dawn was just beginning to lighten the eastern sky as he padded through a dark forest of towering pines and hemlocks. The forest gradually thinned to scattered groves of trees, and soon

Samson was in a wild parkland through which a little river meandered, boiling over huge rounded boulders as it sang its way toward the great valley far below.

The sun was rising with streamers of red and gold as Samson headed toward a sheer granite cliff over which a foaming cataract tumbled in a free fall of thousands of feet. Samson had entered the Valley of Ahwanee — the place of the grizzly bear. There he would stake out his home. Today the area is known as Yosemite.

Summer was a time of plenty in the mountains and Samson had little trouble getting enough to eat. Every sunlit meadow offered a feast of blackberries, elderberries, or buffalo berries, and the young bear gorged on them until he could eat no more. Then he dug for roots or bulbs or insect grubs.

One evening he challenged a mountain lion for a share of the lion's prey, a mule-deer fawn. But the big cat was an experienced old male and was

not about to be intimidated by a bumbling year-ling bear. Eyes blazing and ears laid back, the lion crouched over its prey, its long tail twitching slowly back and forth. When Samson came closer, the lion slashed out with its razor-sharp claws, ripping deep bloody furrows in Samson's side. Yowling with pain, the inexperienced young bear retreated.

His shaggy winter coat was coming out in patches these days, and his tender skin felt itchy as the new fur began to grow in. Samson wallowed

in the mud along the river, plastering himself with a protective layer against the mosquitoes. He rubbed his back against trees to relieve the tormenting itch. Sometimes he rolled over and over in the cool waters of the river.

As fall approached, the nights gradually became colder, and the green-growing meadows of summer turned brown. Now aspens glowed with gold, and the leaves of the dogwoods turned crimson. The oaks began to drop their acorns, and the pine trees were loaded with ripening cones.

Pine squirrels worked from sunrise to sunset, gnawing off pine cones and harvesting seeds from them. Chipmunks and golden-mantled ground squirrels scurried back and forth, filling their cheeks with the seeds and burying them in secret caches under rocks or fallen logs. When Samson uncovered one of these caches, he had a feast.

He filled up on ripe acorns too, as did squirrels and wood rats, jays and woodpeckers. The tireless California woodpeckers drilled hundreds upon hundreds of holes in neat close rows in tree trunks, then carefully stored an acorn in each hole for winter use.

One day Samson rounded a clump of chaparral and came face-to-face with three Indian women, each with a basket at her side. They had been collecting acorns too. Samson and the squaws stared at each other for a moment. Then the women scurried off in one direction, Samson in the other.

The days grew cooler and the nights often left a silvery coating of frost in the meadows. Winter

came earlier at this altitude than it did in the valleys and foothills far below. Samson began to search for a good place in which to spend the winter. He finally chose a natural cave with a narrow opening under a ledge. After enlarging and deepening the den, he dragged leaves and branches into it to make a comfortable bed. When the first snowstorm whirled across the valley, Samson was curled up and asleep in his winter retreat.

Not until mid-April did he emerge from the den and take up the hunt for food once again. Samson ranged far and wide, digging spring bulbs and cropping the first tender shoots of grass. He rolled boulders aside, searching for beetles and grubs. He waded in the icy waters of the river, and his jaws crunched down on crayfish and trout.

By early summer, when he was two and a half years old, Samson weighed more than 300 pounds. Already he was a good-sized bear. He would be much bigger, however, before he was finished growing.

In his travels Samson often followed bear paths that wound through canyons and beside streams, across mountain meadows and under dense growths of chaparral. Some places in the trails were worn smooth and deep by the pads of countless grizzlies before him. In the lower foothills, the paths skirted the pasturelands of the ranchos, while on the high slopes some trails extended past the timberline and into the high craggy regions of almost perpetual snow and ice.

Other grizzlies, as well as black bears, lived in and around the Valley of Ahwanee, and Samson sometimes met them here and there. He usually ignored young bears of his size, unless they tried to share his food. Then, whoofing and bluffing indignantly, the two sparred with each other until the bigger one drove the other away. Often Samson had to run from older male grizzlies that chased him or from protective females with cubs. Grizzlies may be jealous of their home territories, and the bigger the bear the bigger its home territory.

But Samson was growing bigger too. By the time he was four years old he weighed nearly 600 pounds. At five years, he topped 750 pounds. Even for a California grizzly, he was large. In June of that year Samson came upon the scent of a strange grizzly bear one morning while he was eating wild strawberries in a mountain meadow. He immediately started to follow the fresh scent, and after several hours he found the other bear digging bulbs beside the banks of a small stream. The newcomer was a young female grizzly.

She whoofed with surprise when she saw Samson. As he came closer she snarled, then wheeled and loped away as fast as she could go. Samson trailed

her at a distance. He wanted to join the young female, not drive her away.

Mile after mile Samson followed the smaller bear. From time to time she stopped to rest or feed, always snarling at Samson whenever he tried to come closer to her. But in the late afternoon she finally allowed Samson to touch noses with her. Still, she turned away as before and started off. That night she bedded down by herself in a patch of chaparral, growling a warning as Samson tried to creep closer. Samson stopped and lay down some distance away.

At dawn the pursuit continued, but by mid-afternoon the female seemed to be more tolerant of

Samson's presence. Now she allowed him to walk beside her.

Toward dusk Samson heard a growl behind them. Turning, he saw another big male grizzly coming out of a nearby grove of trees. The stranger was about the same size as Samson. He was challenging Samson for the female bear. Samson rumbled angrily as he made ready to fight.

Snarling, the stranger rose on his hind legs as Samson started toward him. Samson broke into a

run and abruptly the challenger dropped to all fours to face him. In a moment the two huge bears were rolling over and over in the meadow, snarling and roaring as they bit and tore at one another. Samson felt his opponent's claws raking his sides, his sharp teeth sinking deep into his shoulder.

Groping for the other bear's throat, Samson ground his own teeth deep into the enemy's furry hide. At the same time he wrapped his forelegs around the challenger's body in a powerful bear hug and dug bloody furrows in his back.

The stranger shrieked in pain as he twisted free, blood flowing from numerous wounds in his body. Samson lunged at him again, and the other ran away as fast as he could go. For a few moments Samson followed him, but soon turned and went back to the meadow where the female waited.

Stalking up to her, he grunted and they touched noses. That evening he mated with her. Seven months later, in her winter den, she would give birth to their cubs.

5   A TASTE OF MUTTON

By the time he was six years old Samson weighed
1,000 pounds — half a ton. At seven years, his
weight was 1,100 pounds. He was fast approaching
his prime, the peak of his strength and power. He
never ran away from another male grizzly anymore.
Instead he chased the other bear away, just as bigger bears once had chased him.

Samson paid little attention to the many black
bears that lived in the Valley of Ahwanee. They
usually kept out of his way or beat a hasty retreat

whenever they saw him. They had one great advantage over Samson: their sharp curved claws. With such claws, a black bear could climb quickly into a tree whenever it was threatened. Samson was unable to follow, for he could not climb. His five-inch claws were much longer than those of the smaller black bears, but they had little curve or point to them. They were useful for digging, but not for hauling Samson's vast weight into a tree.

Here and there along the trails were trees that Samson marked. Standing as high as he could reach, he clawed the bark or tore out a chunk with his teeth, leaving a sign that served as a signal to other bears that he had passed. He was establishing the boundaries of his home territory as he traveled it year after year.

Samson had no fear of any of the wild animals in his domain. The occasional Indians he met were no threat either. He tried to avoid only the vaqueros, with their horses and reatas, their rifles and revolvers.

Samson came into contact with vaqueros and other white men very seldom, however. Sometimes during his rare visits to the lower limits of his territory he sensed their presence. Then he sniffed at the trail odors of men and horses and cattle, and he growled softly to himself.

If any vaqueros were nearby he usually took care to avoid the herds of long-horned cattle that ranged over the lower foothills. But now and then he killed a fat calf or bullock if he was sure the herd was unguarded. Dragging the carcass with

his teeth, he quickly made off with it into the concealing chaparral. There he feasted on it at his leisure.

Once, when he was carrying off a yearling heifer that he had killed, a great black bull with long flaring horns came charging toward him. Dropping his victim, Samson turned to face the bull. As he did so he heard distant shouts, then saw horsemen approaching. Hastily he retreated into the thorny chaparral where neither the vaqueros nor the bull could follow.

The spring and summer of 1847 were very dry, and the grass in the hot lowlands quickly shriveled and died. Shepherds from the ranchos in the San Joaquin Valley led their flocks into the mountains, where the vegetation was still fresh and green. Following the banks of the rivers, the shepherds and bleating flocks wandered higher and higher. Like locusts, the sheep ate everything green in their path and cropped the grass right down to its roots.

When he first came across the broad trail of one of the flocks, Samson followed it curiously. Sheep were something new in his domain. After a few hours he caught up with the fat woolly creatures and watched them from a concealing thicket of scrub oak. That night he killed a big ewe and ate it.

The flock provided good food for the taking, and Samson quickly developed a taste for mutton. He killed another sheep two nights later and carried it away. Frightened, the rest of the flock scattered in all directions. The shepherds spent most of the next day rounding them up.

The two shepherds caught a glimpse of Samson for the first time at dusk several days later. After one horrified look at his great size, they quickly abandoned the flock and climbed into trees. Ignoring them, Samson took another sheep and made off with it.

When Samson went looking for another meal of mutton a few days afterward, the sheep were gone. The frightened shepherds had retreated back to

the lowlands with their flock. Following their
trail, Samson finally came to the carcass of a sheep
in a meadow. After circling and sniffing suspiciously, he began to eat the meat. He was hungry.

When he was satisfied, he dragged the remainder
of the sheep under a dense stand of manzanita.

Scraping dirt and leaves over it, he cached it for a later meal. Then he lay down for a snooze.

After a few minutes he began to feel sharp stabbing pains inside him. They increased, and soon he was roaring with agony. During the next hour he rolled over and over many times, snapping at his sides in desperation and snarling with pain and frustration. Too weak and wracked with agony to do more, he at last lay on his side in the chaparral, wheezing and panting. The mutton he had eaten had been dosed with poison.

Hours later he roused himself enough to stagger to a nearby stream where he drank long and thirstily. He was still very weak, and stabbing pains continued to course through his body. Again he lay down. Twenty-four hours passed before he struggled to his feet once more and made his way into the meadow. There he cropped a few blades of grass. He was beginning to recover.

For the rest of his life Samson never again made a meal from a dead sheep.

56

6 GOLD HUNTERS IN EL DORADO

By the spring of 1849, when he was eight years old, Samson weighed 1,250 pounds. He was a giant bear by now, measuring more than eight feet in length and nearly four and a half feet in shoulder height. His fur was long and thick, a warm red-brown coat that rippled in waves over the muscles that powered his mighty frame. Tipped with five-inch claws, his huge forepaws could strike down an elk with one quick blow or rip a wolf open from end to end.

Samson now ranged over a territory more than twenty-five miles long and half that wide. His hunting grounds included almost the entire valley of the Merced River from its headwaters high in the mountains to the lower foothills.

He seldom encountered men in this vast area. The Indians kept out of his way and never bothered him. They knew that their puny bows and arrows stood little chance against him. As for white men, very few of them ever ventured into the higher reaches of Samson's wilderness domain. Events were taking place, however, that were bringing this isolation to an end.

In February of the previous year, 1848, Mexico had ceded California to the United States after being defeated in war. Gold was discovered about the same time at Sutter's Mill on the American River, little more than 100 miles from the Valley of Ahwanee. When news of the gold strike reached the rest of the world, eager adventurers and fortune hunters began to head for California. The

Gold Rush was on, and Samson's wild homeland would never again be the same.

Early in the summer of 1849, Samson had his first encounter with the newcomers. He was fishing in the shallows of the river one sunny morning when he heard a shout from around the next bend. Climbing ashore, he padded slowly forward, listening for other sounds and sniffing the air for a scent of the intruders. When he rounded the bend, he saw two men wading in the shallows of the river about fifty feet ahead. Each of them had a flat metal pan in his hand. They were prospectors hunting for gold.

When they saw Samson, the two forty-niners splashed their way ashore as quickly as they could and snatched up their rifles from the bank. Samson reared up on his hind legs and watched curiously as they edged away from him. Finally he dropped back to all fours. Voicing an indignant whoof, he turned and headed back the way he had come.

Every week brought other gold hunters to the Sierra Nevada that summer, and Samson began to cross their paths with increasing frequency. One day he came upon two forty-niners walking single file beside the river, each with a rifle in his hand and a pack on his back. The second man was leading a donkey loaded with equipment.

As soon as he saw Samson, the leading prospector raised his rifle and fired it at him. *Whang!* Samson felt the puff of air as the ball whined

past his head. Then the second man fired, and this time the ball buried itself in Samson's shoulder.

The grizzly roared with surprise and pain. Then, before either of the prospectors had time to reload their weapons, he charged them. After one startled look at the giant bear rushing toward them, both men dropped their guns and ran for the nearest trees as fast as they could go. Braying with excitement, the donkey galloped into the brush.

61

The first prospector swung himself into the lower branches of a big oak tree and swiftly climbed out of Samson's reach. But the second man was not so lucky. He stumbled over a root and fell just as he was within reach of safety. By the time he scrambled to his feet again, Samson was almost upon him.

Desperate, the prospector leaped for the lower branches of the tree and started upward. Rearing to his hind feet, Samson struck at the climber with his forepaw. His long claws just grazed the

man's leg, ripping his breeches and tearing off one of his boots. With a terrified shout the prospector scrambled upward out of reach.

For the next hour Samson paced back and forth underneath the two treed men, snarling with rage and frustration. His shoulder wound was beginning to stiffen and throb, and he was in an ugly mood. He chewed at the trees in his anger and tore the captured boot to ribbons.

In the late afternoon the report of a gun sounded in the distance, and then Samson heard faint shouts. The two treed prospectors shouted as loudly as they could in response, and the distant voices called back. Help was on the way. Soon Samson heard the voices much nearer at hand. Growling with frustration, he abandoned his vigil and retreated into the woods. The wound in his shoulder was painful, but it would heal soon.

A few days later, Samson headed for one of his favorite berrying grounds—a mountain meadow beside a small lake where the blackberries were

particularly thick and juicy. But when he got
there, the first thing he saw was a log cabin newly
erected in the middle of the glade. Gold hunters
had moved right into the heart of Samson's
territory.

Standing in the bushes at the edge of the clearing, Samson examined the cabin carefully for
some time, waiting for any movement or activity
around it. There was no sign of life. Satisfied, he
finally padded into the meadow and circled the
cabin. All was still quiet. Sniffing at the pegged
door, he detected the scent of the prospectors who
had built the cabin. But they were not there.
Samson could smell many other things in the
cabin too — things good to eat: bacon and apples
and bread and sugar.

Ripping the door from its hinges, Samson entered the cabin. The first object he saw was a big slab of bacon hanging from a rafter. Pulling it to the floor, he quickly bolted it down. Then he ransacked the interior of the cabin, eating the food supplies and tearing the furnishings apart. He splintered the bunks and shredded the blankets. He reduced the table and rude chairs to kindling, and scattered the pans. Finally satisfied that there was nothing more to eat in the cabin, he walked outside.

As he was leaving the meadow, he heard a distant shout. Then two shots rang out, but the balls fell far short of him. Samson loped into the underbrush where he was hidden from sight.

Several times that day and the next Samson smelled the hated scent of man as he wandered about in his search for food. He was being followed. Uneasy, he kept on the move, and by the next morning he was far away in another section of his territory. Then he smelled a new odor that made him forget everything else — that of a female grizzly. She was close by, and the scent indicated that she was ready to mate. Samson did not take long to find her.

A few days later the two bears were ambling across a clearing when they came to a huge live oak tree with a haunch of venison hanging from one of its lower limbs. Samson was suspicious and hung back, but his mate felt no such hesitation. Lumbering forward, she seized the meat in her teeth and tugged at it. Suddenly there was a loud snap, and the female bear cried out with surprise and pain. Huge metal jaws had closed around her left hind leg, holding it fast. She was caught in an iron bear trap.

Roaring with pain, the female grizzly tried to hobble away. But the harder she pulled, the deeper the cruel spikes cut into her mangled leg. The trap was attached to the trunk of the tree by a stout chain. The woods echoed with roars as the trapped female snapped and clawed at the metal

jaws. They held fast, however, and Samson could do nothing to help her. Exhausted at last, she lay panting on the ground.

The torture continued for two days as the bear struggled hour after hour to free herself. Samson remained nearby, watching and waiting. By dawn of the third day the female was quite weak. She lay groaning on the ground while Samson dozed in a nearby patch of chaparral.

Once again the female bear tugged at the trap in another attempt to free herself. Crazed with pain and frustration, she turned and bit savagely at the chain. As she did so, a gray-bearded hunter dressed in buckskins came out of the forest. Approaching to within a dozen feet of the trapped bear, he raised his rifle, took careful aim, and fired.

The report of the gun woke Samson. The first thing he saw, not thirty feet away, was the bearded hunter. Snarling, Sampson sprang out of the brush and charged.

Completely surprised, the hunter whirled and saw the great bear looming over him. There was no chance for him to escape. Before he could take a step Samson knocked him to the ground with one blow, his claws tearing through the buckskin jacket and raking deep bloody furrows in the man's shoulder and leg.

Growling ferociously, Samson stood over the fallen hunter. Then, seizing him by the shoulder, he shook his victim as a dog would shake a rat, and started to drag him into the brush. After a moment he dropped the limp body and sniffed at it suspiciously.

The hunter lay motionless, his eyes closed, the blood slowly dripping from his shoulder where Samson had mauled him. Samson wrinkled his nose in disgust at the hated man-smell and growled. But the body seemed to be lifeless and

therefore held no further interest for him. Snorting, he left his victim and walked over to where his trapped mate lay.

She was on her side, her eyes glazed, blood dripping from her nostrils. The rifle ball had entered her brain, killing her instantly. Samson nosed her several times, then stood beside her for a few minutes. Finally he turned and left this meadow of death.

An hour later the wounded hunter regained consciousness. He stirred feebly and groaned. Then he remembered what had happened and lay still, scarcely daring to breathe until he was sure that Samson had gone. At last he crawled slowly over to his rifle and reloaded it. He realized that he was lucky to be alive.

Crawling and hobbling, he made his way back to his cabin. There he set about cleaning and binding his wounds. While he did so, he vowed that he would get Samson if it was the last thing he ever did.

7 THE LOG TRAP

One afternoon in late October, four months later, Samson was foraging for acorns in an oak grove when he came upon a strong scent of meat. The body of a deer had been dragged through the trees at this spot. Samson sniffed at the trail and rumbled softly to himself. Mixed with the deer smell were several other scents: wolf and mountain lion — and man.

Following the trail, Samson padded through the oaks and around the edges of a small clearing.

Among the trees on the other side he came to a big boxlike structure made of logs. Built between two huge pine trees, and securely fastened to them, the box was about twelve feet long, five feet wide, and five feet high. It was open at both ends. Samson could see a whole side of venison hanging from the roof inside.

Sniffing greedily, Samson slowly circled the structure and examined it from every side. He was hungry, but experience had taught him to be cautious. This box had been built by men, and men usually meant trouble. It looked something like the cabin he had raided early in the summer.

The giant box was a trap, however. It was constructed on the same principle as a box trap for rabbits, but was intended for grizzly bears. Samson in particular was the target.

Samson, of course, did not know what the structure was. Also, he was hungry. He eyed the venison and licked his lips. The scent of the meat was very tempting.

Making up his mind, he walked into the box. He seized the meat in his jaws and tugged at it, triggering the trap. With a sound of falling timbers the heavy log doors crashed down at either end, trapping Samson inside.

Startled, Samson pushed at the barrier suddenly placed in front of him. The door was almost ten inches thick, however, and held firm. Then he struck the door a heavy blow, tearing out great slivers of wood. But the door did not yield. Again he tried to force his way out, with no success. Each new frustration made him angrier and more violent.

Roaring with rage, Samson chewed and clawed at the door with furious energy. Again and again he flung himself at the sides of his prison, attempting to tear the logs apart. But the log trap took everything he could give it that night and stayed intact.

At dawn, as Samson peered out between cracks in the logs, he saw two men approaching. One of them was young and red-haired. The other was the gray-bearded hunter that Samson had left for dead months before. When this man saw Samson inside the trap, he shouted with excitement. Here was the prize he had hoped to catch.

Samson began to roar as the men approached, and then hurled himself against the log sides of his prison. The whole structure shook with his frenzied assault.

The approaching hunters were alarmed by Samson's violence. If he kept battling, he might break out. Working quickly, they built a huge bonfire beside the trap. When Samson became violent again, they thrust firebrands at his face to make him stop attacking the sides of the trap. At the same time they started to reinforce the structure with additional timbers.

The unequal struggle continued for four long days, until Samson was worn down at last. He did not eat anything in all this time, for ever since his capture he had ignored the venison in the trap. All he had swallowed was a little water from a pan thrust under the door. On the fifth day, however, he bolted down a few chunks of fresh meat that the hunters offered him. The following day the gray-bearded hunter went away, leaving his younger companion to guard Samson by himself.

When the older man returned a week later, he brought two other men with him, as well as a yoke of oxen and a wagon. On the wagon bed rode a big cage made of heavy planks. Lined with metal, the cage was a solid box except for doors at each end made of closely set iron bars.

The four men spent the rest of the day getting ready to transfer Samson from the log trap to the cage. First, they placed the new cage beside the log trap, end to end. Then they securely bound the two together with ropes and chains.

Early the next morning the barred cage door facing the trap was hoisted up, and one of the teamsters stationed himself on top of the cage

to hold and control it. At the same time the older hunter climbed onto the top of the log trap to direct operations. Pulling on a rope levered over a tree limb, the oxen raised the heavy log door of the trap. The way was clear for Samson to leave the log trap and enter the cage.

But Samson would not move. Snarling and sullen, he lay down facing the other way. The men poked rods at him and thrust burning brands at his face as they tried to force him to move. But Samson hunkered down and would not budge an inch, no matter what they did.

After several hours the gray-bearded hunter tried another tactic. With some difficulty he managed to get a loop of chain between the log side and the floor of the trap and around Samson's hind leg. He then passed the end of the chain through the open door of the trap and out through the iron bars of the cage. The oxen were promptly hitched to this end of the chain.

With the yoke of oxen pulling on one side, and the hunters poking with iron rods on the other, Samson felt himself being dragged backwards inch by inch. He roared with anger and clawed at the floor of the log trap, struggling to remain where he was. But the two oxen moved him slowly into the metal-lined box. Finally the heavy barred door of the cage slammed down in front of Samson's nose and was locked shut. The transfer had been accomplished.

The next morning, as soon as the cage had been loaded onto the wagon, the party broke camp and started the long journey down the slopes. The men followed the primitive trail that they had cut on their way up. Now they were heading back to the mining town of Golconda. There the hunters planned to match Samson against a bull in a newly built arena.

Hour after hour the wagon made its tortuous way down the rugged mountainside. As the wagon lurched and jolted its way over the rough trail, Samson hurled himself against the sides of the cage in renewed and frenzied attempts to escape. But all his struggling was in vain. Exhausted by his efforts, he lay down and peered out through the iron bars. High over the slopes behind him a golden eagle was soaring. Bruised in body and spirit, the imprisoned bear finally dozed.

Shouts soon awakened him. The wagon was making its way across a shallow stream where a party of prospectors was working. Several were panning for gold in the riffles. Three others were operating a Long Tom—a twenty-foot wooden trough used to separate gold from water and mud.

There were canvas tents on the banks and cooking fires. One prospector had struck it rich on this stream just a few days before. The news had traveled fast.

The hunters camped halfway down the slopes that evening but were on their way again at dawn the next day. They passed another mining camp, and then a party of loggers busy cutting down trees. The Gold Rush was changing the face of the land very quickly.

By late afternoon they were in the lower foothills. They passed great flocks of bleating sheep, and soon Samson heard cattle bawling. He growled

as four vaqueros galloped up to stare curiously at him. Not long afterward the caravan stopped for the night in the courtyard of a small rancho. Within a few minutes the wagon was surrounded by a chattering group of Mexicans and Indians who wanted to see the huge caged bear. Several of them poked long sticks at Samson, then laughed uproariously as he snarled and slapped at his tormentors. Lean dogs circled about, the hair stiff on their necks as they sniffed and growled at him.

Darkness fell and the onlookers drifted away, one by one. Finally Samson dozed, twitching and rumbling softly to himself in his sleep.

8   THE BEAR-AND-BULL FIGHT

On they went the next day toward the mining
town of Golconda, where Samson's captors had
contracted to enter him as the main attraction in a
gala bear-and-bull fight the following Sunday.
By midafternoon the hunters were within sight
of the canvas tents and rude temporary huts that
marked the eastern outskirts of the town. A half
hour later they were making their way down the
rutted main street toward the newly constructed
amphitheater.

82

Less than twelve months before, this spot had been a wilderness — a wide meadow with scattered groves of oak trees. Through it ran a small creek bubbling down from the surrounding hills. Then gold was discovered in the creek, and within three months the meadow was the site of a rip-roaring mining town that kept growing bigger every day.

That afternoon the main street was swarming with activity. The rainy season had just begun, and on all sides teamsters shouted and cursed at one another as they maneuvered their mules or oxen through the deep mud. Vaqueros galloped down the street, and miners in bright flannel shirts and broad-brimmed hats stopped to stare as the wagon with Samson trundled by them. A muddy stagecoach rumbled past, and then a great canvas-covered Conestoga wagon filled with newly arrived gold hunters hove into view.

Beyond the wooden sidewalks on either side, the street was lined with buildings — saloons and liquor shops, eating places, boarding houses, and stores of every kind. Some Mexicans sat at a sidewalk table playing cards. Next to them a party of miners was drinking and gambling in front of a saloon. When the miners spotted the wagon with Samson, they cheered and raised their bottles in a toast.

Finally the wagon lumbered into the amphitheater, and Samson's cage was unloaded in the center of the ring. The younger of the two hunters fed Samson, and then settled down to guard him while the older mountain man hurried off. Sunday was just two days away, and many arrangements still had to be made before the bear-and-bull fight took place.

The next day posters printed in bright red ink appeared all over town, advertising the contest:

The Fight of the Century! Great Battle!
Just captured,
the biggest bear in California
SAMSON
weighing 1500 pounds
will fight the celebrated black bull
DIABLO
the grizzly killer
on Sunday the 15th inst. at 2 P.M.
at the Golconda Amphitheater
Samson will be chained with a 20-foot chain

Soon after dawn on the day of the contest, the two hunters fastened one end of a twenty-foot chain to a thick post in the middle of the ring. The other end of the chain was fed beneath the door of the cage and locked around Samson's right hind leg just above the huge hairy foot.

Some time before noon Samson heard scuffles under the stands that surrounded the arena, mixed with shouts and bellows. Vaqueros were at work putting his opponent, the bull Diablo, into his holding pen.

About eighty feet in diameter, the central arena was bounded on all sides by a stout log fence almost five feet high. At two places there were barred doors that connected with box stalls under the stands where the fighting bulls were kept. Stretching upward in all directions from the top of the fence were the seats for spectators. They were built in tiers, and supported underneath by a framework of scaffolding.

The crowds began to gather shortly after noon, and many thirsty miners soon were clustered around a bar under the stands. Others began to climb the stairs to their seats. At one end of the arena a three-piece band — violin, banjo, and drums — began to beat out a lively tune. At the other end a clown and tame pig started to go through a series of tricks. In a little while there would be a bull-baiting exhibition, complete with picadors and a matador to finish off the beast.

Shaggy miners with high boots and bright red or blue shirts made up over half of the audience. Most of them were Americans, but forty-niners from France and England and other countries could be seen as well. Many Mexicans were in the crowd too, all of the men dressed in their Sunday finery — woven shirts, gaily patterned vests, and wide sombreros. Here and there were a few Indians in blankets, Chinese with long pigtails, dusky Hawaiians and Malayans, and a noisy group of Australian sailors from a whaling vessel that had been abandoned in San Francisco Bay.

The crowd grew louder and more boisterous as the time of the main bout approached. Many bets in gold nuggets and bags of gold dust as well as paper money were placed. The bull Diablo had killed many bears and was famous. But he had never before met a bear as big as Samson.

At two o'clock the arena was cleared of everything except Samson and his cage. The feature attraction was about to begin. After unlocking the door to Samson's cage, the gray-bearded hunter hoisted it up from a distance, using a rope and pulley. Then a team of horses dragged the cage out from under Samson and over to the fence, dumping Samson onto the ground. Chained to the center post, the giant bear tore up the sod and growled his displeasure. The crowd roared with anticipation when they saw how big he was. Such a bear should put on a good show.

At last the door to the holding pen was opened, and the great black bull exploded from it with a wild rush. But when Diablo saw Samson he stopped stock-still, heaving and snorting as he looked at his opponent. Then, rolling his eyes defiantly, he lowered his head and bellowed. Samson crouched ready at the end of his chain as the huge bull pawed the ground some twenty feet away from him. Diablo was big and heavy, with a coal-black hide as sleek and shiny as satin. His sharp horns, each two feet long, curved out from his head and forward, bending like the tips of a bow.

The bull pawed at the ground for several minutes while he made up his mind what to do. Suddenly, with a quick toss of his head, he charged. Bracing himself, Samson met the attack head on and felt one of the sharp, flaring horns rip at his side. At the same time Samson gave his opponent a blow with his paw that would have broken the neck of a lesser beast — but not this bull. Diablo staggered back, dazed though still on his feet. He shook his head to clear away the blood that streamed from a deep cut on his nose. Samson, too, was bleeding from the thrust of Diablo's horn. The crowd whooped its approval at seeing the two fighters bloodied so quickly.

After a moment Diablo charged a second time and gored Samson in the shoulder, knocking him off balance. Sensing his momentary advantage, the bull thrust downward with all his strength in a lightning attempt to rip the grizzly's belly open. Samson twisted aside just in time, then seized Diablo's head in a fierce hug, raking it with his

claws. At the same time he clamped his teeth firmly on the other's nose.

Diablo bellowed with pain as he tore himself free. Staggering, he moved out of range and stood panting hoarsely. His sides were heaving and the blood was streaming from his nose and shoulders. He was fighting for his life just as Samson was.

Shaking his head once more, Diablo charged back with a rush, his tail high in the air. The crowd roared as the two great beasts tangled again. Samson crouched low trying to seize the bull's

92

head in his huge paws, while Diablo thrust his
horns downward in a deadly twisting sweep. As
Samson rolled sideways to parry the blow, the tip
of one of the bull's horns caught in a link of the
chain that held the bear. There was a sudden loud
snap as the chain broke, and Samson rolled free.

The spectators gasped when they realized what
had happened. Then pandemonium broke out as
the bull and bear crashed against the arena fence.
There was a loud sound of splintering wood, and
a gaping hole appeared.

Crazed by the general confusion, Diablo charged from one side of the arena to the other, goring at the fence and snorting angrily at the screaming crowd. Several vaqueros tossed their lariats at him while a couple of miners shot their revolvers into the air.

Ignoring the uproar, Samson headed for the hole in the fence and quickly scrambled through. Spectators screamed with fright and scattered in every direction. Intent only on escape, Samson paid no attention to anyone, except for a drunken miner whom he brushed aside with a sweep of his paw. Running on through the framework of scaffolding, he burst into the open. Behind him he heard more shouts, more splintering of wood. Then Diablo thundered out and into the clear.

In a moment both animals were on the main street of the town. Diablo ran for the open range, while Samson headed in the opposite direction. Horses whinnied and reared, and people scurried in every direction, like leaves in a whirlwind.

Several men fired their revolvers at him, but Samson continued to head for the hills just as fast as he could go.

Far in the distance, their snowy summits gleaming pink in the rays of the afternoon sun, the craggy peaks of the Sierra Nevada beckoned to him.

AUTHOR'S NOTE

This story of Samson is fiction, but many of the incidents in it are based on historic fact. Numerous records of vaqueros lassoing grizzly bears in the old days are recorded in the book *California Grizzly*, by Tracy I. Storer and Lloyd P. Tevis, Jr. (1955). The account of Samson's capture in a log trap, transfer to a cage, and transport down the mountainside by oxcart is based upon a true incident, as related by Theodore H. Hittell in his 1861 book, *The Adventures of James Capen Adams, Mountaineer and Grizzly Bear Hunter of California*. The bear-and-bull fight in which Samson and Diablo escape parallels the report of an actual contest, as printed in the San Francisco *Daily Alta California* for July 27, 1854. Headlined "Grand Tragi-Comedy at Iowa Hill," the newspaper story relates how both the bear and the bull broke loose and escaped from the arena.

The cruel sport of bear-and-bull baiting continued in California through the 1850's and 1860's but was eventually discredited and prohibited. Ranchers still hunted and killed grizzlies, however, for they were a menace to their cattle and sheep—and occasionally to themselves. The hordes of gold hunters and immigrants who followed them hunted the bears just as eagerly—for sport, for meat, for hides, and simply to get rid of the "varmints." By the 1870's the once-abundant California grizzly bear was fast becoming a rare animal.

By the dawn of the twentieth century grizzly bears had disappeared nearly everywhere in the Golden State. A few still persisted in Yosemite and in several other wilderness areas of the Sierra Nevada, but they were hunted down relentlessly and shot, one by one. The last recorded kill of a California grizzly occurred in 1922. The last one ever sighted in the state was in Sequoia National Park in 1924.

California, the state that celebrates the golden bear on its state flag, had allowed the grizzly to be exterminated within its borders.

CALIFORNIA REPUBLIC